Danish Cookery

by

SUSANNE

Andr. Fred. Høst & Søn
BOOKSELLERS TO H. M. THE KING
COPENHAGEN

© Høst & Søns Forlag 1950. Printed in Denmark by S. L. Møllers Bogtrykkeri, Copenhagen. Cover designed by Vibeke Lind. 10th edition 1974.

ISBN 87 14 27492 2

Frontispiece: Roast pork with the rind on, see page 36

CONTENTS

INTRODUCTION

The Danes enjoy good food and believe that the food they make is good. We believe too that some of our favorite dishes are worthy of notice outside Denmark. This book contains a very modest selection of these. Every effort has been made to avoid including too many dishes which might be found in the cook books of other nations.

For several reasons a Danish cook book cannot give a complete picture of the country's gastronomic joys. Who can describe in a recipe the thrill of the first strawberries, the first new potatoes or the first apples? Breakfast in Denmark is usually a light meal, consisting of bread or rolls and butter, with coffee or tea. If the appetite demands more there is cooked or raw oatmeal with milk and sugar, maybe a boiled egg. In the country dinner is still eaten in the middle of the day, in the towns open sandwiches (the famous *smørrebrød*) are eaten at noon and the hot meal is taken in the evening. Afternoon tea is the exception rather than the rule, but tea or coffee is often taken between 6 p. m. dinner and bedtime. At such times Danish pastries and cookies come into their own.

If the Danish housewife had herself to prepare all the food eaten in her house, she would have little time for anything else. Fortunately she can buy most of the sandwich spreads at a nearby delicatessen store and can always depend on fresh bread, cakes and pastries from the baker. Most bakeries are open most of Sunday, for nobody is interested in eating Saturday's pastries on Sunday.

Maybe some of the dishes in this book will seem so strange that you just cannot muster sufficient courage to try them out. Naturally there is nothing to be done about that. We must take comfort in the thought that there has probably never been a Chinese cook book without recipes for dishes containing swallows' nests. And how do you feel about eating birds' nests anyway?

But, if you have sufficient curiosity, plunge into *"øllebrød"* as well as into *"rødgrød"*. There's always a chance (in the case of the latter, a certainty) that you will not be sorry you tried them out. In any case it is generally through experiment that we gain our most valuable experience. If you agree, we hope that you will have fun and wish you a good appetite.

SOUPS
Suppe

There are many excellent soups native to Denmark. But the Danes like tasty soups and refuse to believe that a good soup can be made with nothing but a few onions, some carrots and a little water. Many of the most popular soups are so rich and strong that they are not intended to appear as first courses only, being a complete meal in themselves.

YELLOW PEA SOUP
Gule Ærter

1⅔ lbs. dried yellow peas
3⅓ lbs. pork, slightly salted or fresh

1 celeriac (if obtainable)
3 carrots
4 leeks
1 lb. potatoes
2 small onions
1 bunch thyme
Mustard

"Gule Ærter" is a winter dish that is a favorite with most Danish husbands. It is made with pork.
Soak 1⅔ lbs. dried, yellow peas in cold, boiled water the day before. Then boil them in 6 cups of the water they were soaked in until they are soft, then strain.
Boil 3⅓ lbs. slightly salted or fresh pork in 3 quarts of water together with celeriac, carrots, leeks, potat-

oes, onions and thyme. Take up the vegetables when they are done and cut them into small pieces. When the pork is tender, take it up and keep it hot; skim the fat from the stock. Add the pea purée and the vegetables to the soup and heat well. Cut the pork in pieces and serve with sour mustard on a separate plate. In Denmark soup and pork are eaten together.

MEAT SOUP WITH VEGETABLES AND DUMPLINGS

Kødsuppe med Urter og Boller

8¾ lbs. beef
7 quarts water
1 celeriac (if obtainable)
4 carrots
5 leeks
½ lb. pork
½ lb. veal
⅔ cup butter
1 cup flour
6 eggs
2 cups milk
Parsley

Put the beef in 7 quarts of water, add salt, cover and boil 10–15 minutes. Then skim and add celery, carrots, leeks and a bunch of the top of a leek, leaves from the celeriac and a sprig of parsley. When meat is tender, remove together with the vegetables, and strain the soup. Cut the vegetables in small pieces. Make *meat balls* as follows: Put veal and pork together through the grinder 4 or 5 times. Add 2 tablespoons of flour, 2 cups of milk and 1 egg. Boil the meat balls by themselves, but do not add to the soup until they are done, otherwise they will thicken the soup.

To make *the dumplings:* Melt ⅔ cup butter, stir in 1 cup flour and add 1 cup boiling water. When mixture is cool, add 5 egg yolks and a little salt and sugar. Finally fold in stiffly beaten egg whites. Form into tiny balls with a teaspoon, drop into boiling water, cook slowly for a few minutes, and remove from water with a perforated spoon. Put the dumplings, the meat balls and the vegetables in the soup and serve. Slice the beef and serve it afterwards with boiled potatoes and horseradish sauce.

GIBLET SOUP
Kraasesuppe

Gizzard, neck, wings, feet, heart of a goose
4 carrots
1 celeriac (if obtainable)
4 leeks
4 peppercorns
2 lbs. apples
½ lb. prunes
½ cup butter
½ cup flour
Sugar
Vinegar

Cut the neck into three pieces, and remove windpipe and gullet. Clean and wash the gizzard, and peel off the thick inside membrane. Cut each wing in two pieces. Remove skin and claws from feet. Wash blood out of the heart. Put all this in a pot with cold water and salt, bring to boil and skim. Add a bunch of the top of a leek and the celeriac leaves, carrots, leeks and peppercorns. Cook for about three hours or until the meat is tender, then strain the soup. Peel and core and slice the apples and combine with prunes, sugar and water. Boil the fruit until this is tender.

Melt butter and stir in flour, gradually add the liquid from the apples and prunes and finally the soup. Add sugar and vinegar to taste. Cut the vegetables and meat in small pieces and add to the soup together with the apples and prunes. Make dumplings (see page 9). Add to soup and serve boiling hot. The soup is in itself a complete meal.

CHERVIL SOUP
Kørvelsuppe

6 cups stock
2 carrots
½ cup butter
⅓ cup flour
4 tablespoons minced chervil

Chervil is a member of the parsley family, but the taste somewhat resembles water cress.

Combine the butter and flour in a pot, add the stock and simmer about 15 minutes. Strip the chervil of the coarsest stalks, rinse and put through the grinder two or three times. Heat the boiled, sliced carrots in the soup and add the chervil just before serving. Do not let it boil or it will lose its delicate flavor and fresh green color. When serving, put a poached egg in each dish.

RICE PORRIDGE
Risengrød

9 cups milk
7 oz. rice
Butter

Rice porridge is a typical Danish Christmas dish, and is served as a first course just before the roast goose.

But it is also very popular as a regular winter dish and is made like this:

Boil the milk and stir in the rice, which has been rinsed in cold water and scalded in boiling water. Stir until the porridge comes to a boil, then put on a tight lid and let it simmer over extremely low heat. Allow to simmer for about an hour and a half, but just before serving add a little more boiling milk if it seems too solid.

To the astonishment of all foreigners, the Danes drink very sweet, non-alcoholic malt beer *(hvidtøl)* with their rice. When serving, put a lump of butter in the center of each plate so that the person eating the rice can dip his spoon in the melting butter at each mouthful.

BREAD SOUP
Øllebrød

10 oz. black rye bread (Danish)

1 cup water
3 cups "Hvidtøl" (malt beer)
Sugar and milk or cream to taste.
1 lemon

Bread soup is so typically Danish that we just cannot omit the recipe. We doubt however it will be possible for you to make it in your own country as both Danish rye bread *(rugbrød)* and a sweet, non-alcoholic malt beer *(hvidtøl)* are necessary ingredients. These you will probably find difficult to obtain outside Denmark.

Øllebrød is a dish as popular in the Danish royal family as it is in humbler homes. You find people eating it at breakfast or dinner all over the country, from the poorest cottage to the King's own palace. Bread soup is a very filling dish. Here, then, is the recipe: Break the bread up into small pieces and soak it for several hours in the mixture of water and beer. Cook over low heat, stirring every now and then, bringing the mixture to a boil. When it has become a thick soup remove it from the fire and strain it through a coarse sieve. Then bring it to a boil again and add sugar, lemon juice and grated rind to taste. Ordinarily we serve it with a dash of milk or cream in each soup bowl, but on special occasions and at the King's palace you'll find whipped cream on top!

FRUIT SOUP
Sødsuppe

Fruit juice
Sugar
Lemon peel
Cinnamon
Sago or tapioca

Hot soup is served in Denmark both as a first and a last course. The most common and easy way is to make the soup of sweet fruit juice. Boil it with 4 oz. sago to 1½ quarts of soup until the grains are transparent. Strips of lemon peel and whole cinnamon can be cooked in the soup. Serve with dumplings (which are so often found in good Danish soups) and with prunes, cooked in the soup, or tiny zwieback which are crushed and put in the plates just before eating the soup.

But there are special kinds of fruit soup too, that deserve further mention, for instance:

ELDERBERRY SOUP
Hyldebærsuppe

1 lb. elderberries
2½ quarts water
Lemon peel
Cinnamon
Sugar

The berries must be quite ripe. Take them off the stems with a fork and cook them in water together with the lemon peel and whole cinnamon. Drain the juice and sweeten with sugar to taste. Thicken and serve hot. Can be served either with quartered cooked apples and dumplings or with cubes of dry white bread fried in butter and sugar.

APPLE SOUP
Æblesuppe

1½ lb. apples
2½ quarts water
Lemon peel
Cinnamon
Sago flour or corn-flour
Sugar

The soup will be best if sour apples are used. Quarter, core, but don't peel the apples. Cook until quite tender in half the amount of water, and add cinnamon and lemon peel to taste. Then rub them through a strainer, add the rest of the water and thicken with sago flour or corn flour mixed with cold water. Allow to cook well after adding the flour. Sweeten to taste, and if desired, a little wine can be added. The soup should be thickened so that it takes on a creamy consistency but don't sweeten so much that the tart flavor of the apples is taken away. Serve hot with zwieback crushed in the plates just before eating.

COLD BUTTERMILK SOUP
Kærnemælkskoldskaal

4 cups buttermilk
2 eggs
4 tablespoons sugar
1 teaspoon vanilla extract
Juice of 1 lemon

Beat the eggs, sugar, lemon juice and vanilla together in the bowl the soup is to be served in. Beat the buttermilk and fold in a little at a time.

If you want to make something out of this dish, top the bowl with 1 cup of whipped cream. Small cakes of oat meal, fried in butter and sugar, pressed into moistened eggs cups and turned onto a plate, are served with this dish.

It can also be served after the main course with whipped cream, meringue and sweetened fruit.

FISH
Fisk

Experts on fish who come to Denmark claim that Danish fish is so good that you have to go all the way to California to find its equal. In any case you can be sure that the Danish fish seller has plenty of good, fresh fish at reasonable prices all year round. The cheapest are cod and herring, besides in summer, garfish, mackerel and catfish. Plaice and eel are a little more expensive, and in the luxury class too you can find wonderful salmon, halibut and trout. In shellfish we have fine lobsters, crabs and crayfish and don't forget to taste our tiny pink shrimps that are something very specially Danish.

PLAICE SURPRISE *Rødspætte surprise*

Plaice is one of the most popular of fishes in Denmark. It is served in a variety of ways, including even cold (after having been first duly rolled in breadcrumbs and fried) as an item of *smørrebrød*. Kill and skin a large plaice (i. e. weighing about 1 lb.). Wash well. Sprinkle with kitchen salt and let

Opposite: Fried eels with creamed potatoes, see page 18 and Jellied eel, page 17

stand for ten minutes, then rinse and dry in a piece of cloth. Turn in flour and then in beaten eggs, roll in bread crumbs and fry, first in pure oil or lard and then in slightly browned butter.

Just before serving, lay a strip of freshly shelled shrimps along the middle of the fish. Serve with spinach steamed in butter and cream, asparagus tips or stewed mushrooms Add a piece of lemon by way of decoration. Serve either browned butter or a light white wine sauce with this festive dish.

JELLIED EEL
Aal i Gélé

1 eel	2 bay leaves
1 onion	Gelatine
4 whole peppercorns	Vinegar

Skin and clean an eel and cut it in pieces from 2 to 3 inches long. Boil it in the amount of water required to fill out your mold (measure in the mold itself) together with salt, a sliced onion, four whole peppercorns and 2 bay leaves.

Remove the eel when it is cooked, drain and cool. Drain the stock, season with vinegar and add gelatine. Wet the mold with a little cold water, pour in some of the stock and when this is stiff put in the pieces of eel mixed with the bay leaves and peppercorns. You can decorate with fresh parsley tops. Pour over the rest of the stock and let the whole thing stand until the gelatine is stiff. Loosen and turn out on a round platter. The mold looks somewhat like an

angel-cake pan but the sizes vary. Danish housewives insist on one with a hole in the middle.
Jellied eel can be served as a dinner course with
cold potato salad, but it is also popular on our open
sandwiches or as one of the dishes which form part
of the "cold-table". (See ill. by page 16).

CURRIED EEL	1–2 eels	1 large onion
Aal i Karry	Parsley	$^1/_3$ cup flour
	1 tablespoon butter	1 scant teaspoon curry

One large or two small eels are suitable for 4 persons. Skin the eel, cut in pieces as long as a finger
and put in boiling salt water with a sprig of parsley.
Use water enough to cover only half the fish, so the
stock will be good and strong. Cook the eel until
it is tender and keep it hot while making the sauce.
Melt butter in a pot, brown a large onion and add
flour and curry. Dilute with the fish stock until the
sauce is thick enough. Taste it, and if it is not strong
enough add more curry. Pour it over the eel, serve
in a deep dish and have an extra dish of fluffy
steamed rice.

FRIED EELS WITH	Eels	Eggs
CREAMED POTATOES	Salt	Breadcrumbs
Stegt Aal med stuvede Kartofler	Flour	Butter

Skin and clean the eels carefully, cut in 3-inch
pieces, sprinkle with salt and leave for an hour. Rinse

and dry thoroughly, dip in flour and a beaten egg, roll in breadcrumbs and fry in plenty of butter. Serve with the browned butter and creamed potatoes.

Creamed potatoes: Melt a tablespoonful of butter, add 1½ tablespoons flour and a little milk. Stir over a low flame until thickened; season with salt and a little sugar. Cut boiled potatoes in small pieces and add' to this sauce. Serve garnished with chopped parsley and butter. When Danish anglers meet to have fried eel, they try to eat so many that the back-bones form a ring around each plate. (Ill. by p. 16).

FRIED HERRINGS AND ONION SAUCE
Stegt Sild med Løgsauce

8 medium sized herrings
2 eggs

Breadcrumbs
4 tablespoons flour
3 large onions, finely chopped
Milk
Salt to taste
Sugar to taste
Butter

Rinse and bone the herrings. Dip in flour (2 tablespoons), the beaten eggs, and the breadcrumbs. Fry in plenty of butter.
Serve with onion sauce and boiled potatoes.
To make the onion sauce melt 2 tablespoons of butter in a pot over a low flame. Stir in 2 tablespoons flour and add milk, keeping mixture smooth. Cook until thickened. Add onions and bring to a boil. (If desired onions may be boiled first in a little water). Season with salt and sugar.

BORNHOLM	6 smoked herrings	Chives
OMELET	8 eggs	Salt
	1 cup milk	1 head of lettuce
Bornholmeræggekage	1 bunch radishes	Butter

This omelet received its name because it is made of the wonderful smoked herrings that come from Bornholm, Denmark's only rocky island.

Beat the eggs and milk together and add the salt. Melt butter in a frying pan and cook the omelet in this over low heat. Stir it a little to begin with as this makes it light and airy, and don't let it harden until just before it is done, and then turn the heat even lower. Bone the smoked herrings and arrange the filets in a star on top of the omelet. Cut the radishes in thin slices and put between the herring pieces. Sprinkle the whole omelet with finely cut chives and lettuce cut in thin strips. Serve the omelet in the pan, steaming hot!

BOILED COD *Kogt Torsk*

Cod is one of the most popular fish in Denmark. We eat it during the months containing the letter R, beginning in September and ending in April.

Scrape and rinse cod thoroughly. Sprinkle with salt and let stand for about 1 hour. If the fish is to be served whole, place in cold water and bring to a boil. If it is to be cut, drop the pieces into boiling water. Boil, uncovered, until done. Serve fish hot with boiled potatoes and plenty of melted butter. If desired, serve also separate dishes of chopped raw onions, pickled beets, chopped hard boiled eggs, finely chopped parsley and grated raw apple.

STEWED CODFISH
Plukfisk

Leftover boiled cod
1 tablespoon butter

Milk or cream
1 tablespoon flour
Salt
Pepper
Thinned mustard (or leftover mustard sauce)
Cold boiled potatoes, diced

Carefully remove bone and skin from leftover boiled codfish and flake into quite small pieces.

Make a smooth white sauce of the butter, flour and milk or cream. Season with salt and pepper, and add the mustard or mustard sauce. Combine the fish, potatoes, and sauce.

KLIPFISH *Klipfisk*

Klipfish is salted dried cod, and Danish klipfish is so good that large quantities of it are exported to Spain, where "bacalao", as it is called there, is much appreciated.

Cut 2 lbs. of fish in pieces and soak for 24 hours in lukewarm water (or milk, if desired) with a teaspoon of soda. Take up the fish, cut off the fins, and scrape the skin. Put over the fire in cold water without salt and cook for half an hour until quite tender.

Serve on a hot platter garnished with parsley and

with boiled potatoes, melted butter, mustard sauce and a dish of diced, hard boiled eggs (figure one egg per person).

FRIED GARFISH (SEA-PIKE) *Stegt Hornfisk*

Clean, bone and halve two garfish, splitting the filets also in halves.

Salt the fish and let stand for 10 minutes. Clean and dry the pieces, roll in flour, beaten egg and bread crumbs (in that order) and fry in plenty of butter.

Serve with browned butter and lemon slices, and with boiled white potatoes.

JELLIED GARFISH *Hornfisk i Gélé*

Clean, bone and cut the garfish in pieces, and jelly as described in recipe for jellied eel, page 17. It looks beautiful if you color the jelly light green by adding a little artificial coloring.

As a dinner course, it will taste delicious with boiled, sliced and fried potatoes and a salad made of tomato slices turned in a dressing made of vinegar and oil.

GARFISH FRIED LIKE CHICKEN
Hornfisk stegt som Kylling

Clean, bone and halve two garfish. Roll a sprig of parsley and a dab of butter inside each filet and hold the rolled pieces together with a sharpened match or a toothpick. Brown butter in a pot, and brown the garfish "chickens" until golden brown all over. Allow to simmer over a low flame for about 5 minutes.

Take up the fish, remove the matches, and keep hot while making the sauce. This is made by thickening the fat with a little flour, stirring in some cream and a little meat stock. Serve this dish with boiled potatoes and lettuce, the sauce in a bowl of its own.

MINCED FISH
Fiskefars

Minced fish
Per lb. minced fish use:
2 tablespoons salt
½ cup butter (scant)
2 tablespoons flour
1 teaspoon pepper
Milk or cream

Pike gives a very fine minced fish but cod or had-dock can also be used for this dish. For very special occasions salmon is exquisite!

Clean, scrape, and bone the fish and mince it with a spoon until it is a fine, smooth mixture. Add salt and keep working at it for a while. Stir butter until very light, then add flour and pepper. At last add the fish and milk or cream until the mixture is soft and mushy. If you are making fish balls, it must not be so soft as when put in a ring mold.

For making balls, drop mixture from large spoon onto a well greased frying pan, fry on both sides. If cooking in ring mold, cover mold with wax paper and place in a pot with boiling water. Cook until set. Fish balls are served with tomato sauce, and fish mold may be garnished with lobster or crab meat and served with Hollandaise sauce.

PARTY FISH *Selskabs Fiskeret*

If you have ever participated in a Danish family party, you will probably be acquainted with this fish course, which is a necessary part of the menu on such occasions.

Arrange alternately boiled and fried plaice to make a ring around a large dish. The fried plaice is sprinkled with flour and dipped in beaten eggs, rolled in bread crumbs, and French fried in lard or fried in butter. The boiled plaice fillets are rolled (as the garfish, page 22) and steamed. In a ring inside the plaice put alternately lobster claws and halved tails and patty shells with creamed spinach. Besides, if you don't mind the expense, you can serve, also in patty shells grilled mussels, boiled asparagus, and mushrooms stewed in cream.

The center of the platter contains a round pudding of boiled fish meat, to be sliced. (See recipe for Minced Fish). Serve with Hollandaise sauce.

VEGETABLES
Grøntsager

Why always depend on meat or fish for a main course? The following recipes show how we Danes like to make our fresh garden vegetables into the more substantial part of a meal.

CAULIFLOWER AND CHEESE SAUCE
Blomkaal med Ostesauce

1 large or two small cauli-
    flower heads
⅛ cup butter
⅓ cup flour
Milk
2 egg yolks
Grated cheese
Sugar
Salt
Breadcrumbs

Boil the cauliflower, and when just about tender remove from water, drain, and place in a baking dish. Melt butter in a pan, add the flour and dilute gradually with enough boiling milk to make a sauce that is not too thin. Take it off, stir in egg yolks, and thereafter grated cheese according to taste. Season with sugar and salt.

Either put the whole heads of cauliflower in the baking dish, or part them in 4 "bouquets". Pour the sauce over them, sprinkle with breadcrumbs and put dabs of butter here and there on top. Put it in a hot oven.

Serve in the same dish when the top is golden brown.

STEWED WHITE CABBAGE
Stuvet Hvidkaal

Small head of cabbage
$1/_8$ cup margarine
$1/_3$ cup flour
Milk
Salt
Pepper

Divide a small head of cabbage into 4 parts and cut out the stalk. Cook the cabbage in salt water until tender. Then take it off and drain.

Make a white sauce of margarine and flour, and enough milk to make a smooth, even sauce. Add the coarsely cut cabbage and season with salt and pepper. Serve with meat balls, boiled ham, or other meat dishes.

STEWED STRING BEANS
Stuvede Snittebønner

String beans
$1/_8$ cup butter
$1/_3$ cup flour
Milk
Parsley
Salt
Sugar

Use string beans so young that the beans themselves have only just begun to form. Remove strings, if any, and cut diagonally. Boil in salt water until tender and drain.

Melt the butter, thicken with flour, and dilute with

enough milk to make a smooth sauce. Season with salt and sugar and add the boiled beans. Sprinkle with diced parsley before serving. Serve with ham, frankfurters or with other meat dishes.

VEGETABLE PATTIES
Grøntsags-Frikadeller

Cooked vegetables
Breadcrumbs
2 whole eggs
Salt
Pepper
Butter

Practically all kinds of cooked vegetables may be used for these "meat balls"– potatoes, cabbage, carrots, celery, or any other kind at hand.

Let the cooked vegetables go once through the grinder, and stir in the breadcrumbs, eggs, salt and pepper, until it becomes sticky and syrupy.–Make round or oval balls of this, dip them in bread crumbs and fry on a pan in plenty of butter. Serve with stirred or melted butter and white bread.

DANISH SOUFFLÉ
Gratin

$\frac{1}{2}$ cup butter
$\frac{2}{3}$ cup flour
$1\frac{1}{2}$ cup boiling milk
5 eggs, separated
Breadcrumbs

The Danes often make soufflés. This is due to the fact that eggs in their country are always fresh and because any kind of vegetables or leftovers may be used in a soufflé.

Melt butter in a pan and stir in flour. Add boiling milk.

Cook, stirring constantly until the mixture thickens.
Take off and stir in egg yolks, one at a time. Season
with a little salt and sugar and fold in the stiffly
beaten egg whites. Sprinkle a buttered baking dish
with breadcrumbs and fill with alternate layers of the
batter and of the filling. Bake about 45 minutes in a
moderate oven, and serve at once. The filling may be
half-boiled pieces of cauliflower, boiled asparagus,
peas, carrots, or other leftover vegetables, sweetbreads, mushrooms, or boiled fish.

CUCUMBER SALAD
Agurkesalat

1 large cucumber
1 cup water
1 cup vinegar
Black pepper to taste
Sugar to taste

In Denmark a "large cucumber" means one about a
foot and a half long; but it is only about an inch and
a half in diameter, has practically no seeds or thorns,
and tastes like any well-grown cucumber.

Wash and dry a large cucumber thoroughly. If it
is a spring cucumber the green rind may be left on,
but later in the season, when the rind is thicker and
harder, it is best to peel the cucumber.

Cut the cucumber into very thin slices with a sharp
knife. Mix the water and the vinegar, and sweeten to
taste. Add the cucumber slices and sprinkle with
pepper. Let stand for an hour or so before serving.

Lemon juice can be used instead of vinegar – this makes the salad healthier for children.

PICKLED RED BEETS *Syltede Rødbeder*

Clean the beets and boil in water until tender. This takes a long time, at least two hours. They can be tested with a knitting needle. Take them out of the water and skin them. Allow to cool, then slice and put them in a crock, sprinkling sugar heavily between each layer. If desired add caraway seeds. Finally add a mixture of vinegar and water well above the top layer.

In 24 hours they **are re**ady to eat and may be served with various kinds of meat and in many kinds of salad.

STEWED RED CABBAGE
Rødkaal

3 lbs. red cabbage
2–4 tablespoons butter
2 tablespoons sugar
1 tablespoon vinegar or $\frac{1}{2}$ lemon
$\frac{1}{2}$–1 cup red currant juice

Remove outer leaves and shred cabbage. Melt butter and sugar in an iron saucepan, add the cabbage, steam a little and add a little water and vinegar. Simmer covered until quite tender (2–3 hours) and stir occasionally. When nearly done add red currant juice and more sugar and vinegar to taste. Caraway seeds or peeled and sliced apples are often added.

Red cabbage is best if prepared the day before it is to be used. Serve with roast loin of pork or roast goose.

MEAT COURSES
Kødretter

Danes love meat! This is probably due to the fact that we produce a lot of meat in this country, and that it is usually first rate. At least "meat dishes" is one of the main chapters in Danish cook books and it is probably in this field that our native sense of invention is most flourishing.

MINCED BEEFSTEAK
Hakkebøf

1 lb. lean beef
Flour
Salt and pepper to taste
4 large onions
Water

Put the meat once through the grinder. Form into 6 flat, round, or oval patties.

Roll each patty in flour, sprinkle with salt and pepper, and fry in butter. Mix the butter in which patties have been fried with a little water, and thicken with a mixture of flour and water. Slice the onions and fry in butter or fat until they are golden brown. If fat is used, drain onions on absorbent paper. Top each patty with browned onions, or add these to the gravy. Serve with boiled potatoes.

MOCK TURTLE
Forloren Skildpadde

1 calf's head	3 tablespoons tomato puree
½ cup butter	Gravy coloring
4 onions	1 cup flour
4 carrots	10 oz. white bread
2 leeks	⅛ cup margarine
1 celeriac	2 eggs
Milk	Salt and pepper
	Madeira
	Meat balls
	Fish balls

In Denmark the preparing of mock turtle is the touchstone of a housewife's ability. It is a complicated dish but one that can be made beforehand and once it is made it's easy to serve and thus suitable for big get-togethers.

Let the butcher split the calf's head. The day before mock turtle is to be served, remove tongue, brain and eyes, and soak the head in cold water for 2 hours. Clean the head and scald it. Cover with cold water, add salt and boil until the meat is loosened from the bones. Pour off water and save. Next day remove the meat from the bones and place it in a bowl. Cover with lid and place heavy weight on top. Later, cut into 1-inch squares. Boil the tongue. Remove skin and cut into 1-inch sq. small meat balls (see pages 8 and 44). Prepare small fish balls (see page 23) or use canned ones. Next make sauce as follows: Brown ½ cup butter. Add sliced onions, carrots, sliced leeks, celeriac and a few of its leaves. Add the water the calf's head was boiled in, together with 3 tablespoons tomato puree and a little brown coloring. Simmer 1½ hours.

Opposite: Mock Turtle

If necessary add a little beef extract. Strain. Melt 3 tablespoons of butter, stir in 3 tablespoons of flour and add to sauce to thicken it. Add Madeira to taste. Combine the meat, tongue, meat balls, fish balls and sauce. Finally make balls with the brain. As these are difficult to handle do not make them until the last moment, and only add to the other ingredients just before serving. Soak the brain in salt water 2 hours; then drain in a fine sieve. Remove the crust from 10 ounces of white bread (it's best if the bread isn't too soft) slice and soak in as much milk as it will absorb for about an hour. Melt $\frac{1}{8}$ cup margarine, add bread and $1\frac{1}{2}$ tablespoons flour. Stir over low heat until the mixture leaves the side of the pot, then pour into a bowl. Into this sieve the brain. Add 2 egg yolks, salt, pepper and stiffly beaten egg whites. Form into small balls with a teaspoon and cook in boiling water or hot fat. Place a halved hardboiled egg per person in the mock turtle. (See illustration opposite p. 32).

STEWED BEEF

Bankekod

$1\frac{2}{3}$ lbs. lean beef
$\frac{1}{3}$ cup butter
2 bay leaves
10 whole peppercorns
4 tablespoons flour

Remove the sinews from the meat, slice it, and pound the slices well. Cut the slices into smaller pieces and season with salt. Then roll in flour and brown in butter in a pot. Pour just enough boiling water into the pot to cover the meat. Add the peppercorns and bay leaves and let simmer until the meat is tender —about an hour and a half. If desired, thicken the gravy with a little flour mixed with cold water but as a rule the flour on the meat will be enough. Serve with Danish-style mashed potatoes. These are thinner than American as much more milk is added.

CALF'S LIVER AND ONION GRAVY
Kalvelever med Løgsauce

1 lb. liver	Flour
Salt	4 large sliced onions
Pepper	Butter
	Milk

Soak the liver for about an hour and take off the skin. Cut in thin slices and sprinkle with salt and pepper. Flour the slices and fry in plenty of butter. When done, keep the liver hot, boil off the frying pan with milk, and pour the drippings into a dish.

Fry the onions in plenty of butter. When browned, sprinkle with one large tablespoon of flour and add the drippings. If stronger gravy is desired, add bouillon. Serve with the gravy poured over the liver and with white boiled potatoes.

BONELESS BIRDS
Benløse Fugle

Round steak, ½ inch thick
Fat pork
Onions
Salt and pepper
2 tablespoons butter

Make two "birds" for each person. Pound slices of the beef well. On each slice put a strip of fat pork, add one teaspoon finely chopped onions, and season with salt and pepper. Roll the beef round the filling, and tie. Brown the butter in a pot, and turn the "birds" in it till they are golden brown. Add boiling water until it just covers the meat, and simmer about two hours, or until "birds" are tender. Thicken the sauce with flour mixed with cold water. Serve with boiled potatoes.

Veal may be used for this recipe instead of beef, in which case, the "birds" are called "mock chickens". Fill with parsley instead of fat pork and onions.

SPAGHETTI WITH SWEETBREADS AND MUSHROOMS

Spaghetti med Brisler og Champignons

6 veal sweetbreads
Vinegar
2 bay leaves
½ cup butter
Flour
½ lb. mushrooms
5 oz. spaghetti

Soak 6 good veal sweetbreads for an hour in water and vinegar, then clean them and boil in salt water with a little vinegar and 2 bay leaves.

Remove, drain and skin the sweetbreads. Cut in small pieces. Melt ½ cup butter in a pan, thicken with flour and dilute with the stock until the gravy is no longer thin. If desired, season with a little more vinegar. Mix in the sweetbread pieces together with ½ lb sliced mushrooms, browned in butter. Finally add the previously boiled spaghetti and serve very hot. In Denmark white bread is eaten with this dish.

FRIED GROUND VEAL AND PORK
Stegte Karbonader

Veal
Pork
Breadcrumbs

Flour
Salt
Butter

Grind equal parts of veal and pork (the latter a little fat) and mix well.

Make oval balls of this, turn them in flour and egg and roll in breadcrumbs and a little flour seasoned with a pinch of salt. Fry on the pan in plenty of butter until the balls are golden brown on both sides. Cook off the pan with cream, and, if desired, add a little meat stock. Serve the gravy in a gravy bowl.

Serve boiled potatoes, or browned potatoes (see page 42) and all kinds of vegetables to this dish.

ROAST PORK WITH THE RIND ON
Flæskesteg med Svær

Fresh ham or loin of pork
Flour
Salt

In Denmark pork is usually roasted with the rind on. Score the rind with a sharp knife lengthwise and crosswise, spacing slits ½ inch apart. Now wash the roast in cold water, rub it thoroughly with salt and put it in a moderate oven. Put water in the bottom of the pan after roast has been in the oven at least 15 minutes, and do not baste the roast or the rind will not be crisp.

Pour the gravy from the roasting pan, thicken with

flour mixed with cold water, add salt, and if necessary a little beef extract. Serve with potatoes fried
in sugar (see page 42) and red cabbage (see page 29).
See illustration on frontispiece.

TENDERLOIN OF PORK WITH APPLES AND PRUNES

Pork tenderloin
Apples
Prunes
Butter

Morbrad med Æbler og Svesker

For 4 persons use 2 tenderloins. Remove sinews, cut
the meat open lengthways. Scald the prunes and
remove the stones. Peel the apples and cut into small
pieces. Stuff tenderloin with fruit and tie. Brown the
meat in butter in a pot, add enough water to cover
the meat and simmer for about half an hour. Thicken
the gravy with a little flour blended with cold water
and serve with boiled potatoes.

BACON AND PARSLEY SAUCE

Stegt Flæsk med Persillesauce

Thinly sliced home-style bacon
Potatoes

2 tablespoons butter
1 tablespoon flour
½ cup milk or cream
Pinch of salt
Pinch of sugar
2 tablespoons finely minced
  parsley

Cut the bacon in thin slices and fry. Serve with boiled
potatoes and parsley sauce. To make the sauce:
Mix 1 tablespoon butter and the flour. Add milk or
cream and cook until thickened. Add salt and sugar.

Just before serving add parsley. After pouring sauce into gravy bowl put the rest of the butter on top.

ROAST LOIN OF PORK WITH APPLES AND PRUNES
Stegt Svinekam med Æbler og Svedsker

Partly separate meat from rib, and stuff with pieces of peeled apple and scalded prunes without stones. Tie the meat together over the stuffing. Roast in a hot oven.

Serve with potatoes fried in sugar (see page 42), thick gravy and red cabbage (see page 29).

PORK AND CABBAGE
Flæsk i Kaal

2 lbs. salt pork or bacon
1 large head of white cabbage

Boil the meat half an hour. Pour off and save all but a little of the water. Place cabbage cut in 8 pieces, around and on top of the meat. Cook covered for about 3 hours or until bacon and cabbage are tender. Stir the cabbage occasionally to prevent burning and if necessary add a little of the broth. Slice the bacon and serve on a platter with the cabbage.

PORK AND BROWN CABBAGE
Flæsk i Brunkaal

1 head of white cabbage
2 tablespoons sugar
2 tablespoons butter
2 lbs. pork spare-ribs, fresh or slightly salted

Divide the head of cabbage into 8 parts and shred coarsely. Caramelize the sugar in a pot over a low flame. Add the butter and brown the cabbage in this. If a deeper color is desired, add a little soy sauce. Add a little water, cover and steam until tender. This will take about 2 hours.

Add the pork in one piece an hour before the cabbage is done. If desired, the pork may be diced, in which case it should not be added until about 35 minutes before the cabbage is done.

PORK AND APPLES
Æbleflæsk

8 slices bacon or slightly salted pork
2 lbs. apples
Sugar

Fry the pork without fat in a hot frying pan until the slices are golden brown and tender, then take them up and keep hot in a dish.

Wash the apples, core and cut them in 8 parts. Fry the apples in the pork fat until they are soft, but not mushy, turn them with care.

When the apples are done, add sugar to taste and put them in a hot dish with the pork slices placed decoratively on top.

GRILLED LAMB'S HEAD *Grilleret Lammehoved*

Figure ½ lamb's head per person. Have the butcher cut them in two. Clean them carefully and soak in salt water for a few hours. Then put on to cook in fresh salt water together with the tongues, and allow to simmer until it is easy to skin them. Peel the skin carefully off both the heads and the tongues. Cut out the eyes and ears (but above all, do not remove the fat behind the eyes) experts claim that tastes best of all. Remove the palate. Split the tongues in two. Dip each piece, both the half heads and half tongues, in beaten eggs, and then in bread crumbs blended with flour and salt. Fry in a pan in plenty of butter and serve with all sorts of vegetables and tiny boiled potatoes, turned in butter.

ROAST GOOSE WITH APPLES AND PRUNES
Gaasesteg med Æbler og Svedsker

The main dish at the Danish Christmas table is roast goose and age–old tradition demands that the goose must be stuffed with peeled and sliced apples and prunes. The goose is roasted as usual after being stuffed and rubbed well with salt. When done, take out some apples and prunes and arrange on the plate around the goose as ornament. Serve with potatoes, browned in sugar (see page 42), and red cabbage.

SAILORS' STEW
Skipperlabskovs

1⅔ lbs. lean beef or veal
3 lbs. potatoes
5 large onions
¾ cup butter
12 whole peppercorns
2 bay leaves

Chop the onions coarsely and cut the meat into cubes. Melt the butter in a pot and turn the meat and onions in the butter, but do not brown them. Add boiling water until the meat is just covered, then add a pinch of salt, the peppercorns, and the bay leaves. Simmer over low heat for about 20 minutes. Peel and dice the potatoes and add to the meat. Now let the mixture cook until the potatoes have been blended with the meat broth, giving the appearance of a very thick potato soup. Take off. Place a dish with small balls of butter on the table so that each portion can be topped with a butter ball. Serve chopped chives in a separate dish.

DANISH HASH
Biksemad

Cold beef (enough to fill a
   soup plate)

2 large onions
1 lb. boiled potatoes
Salt and pepper
Worcestershire sauce or
   tomato catsup
1 egg to each person

This Danish dish is made of leftovers. Brown the meat in butter in a frying pan. Take off and place in a dish. Slice the onions finely, brown in butter, and mix with the meat. Dice the potatoes and brown in butter. Now mix meat, onions and potatoes and return to frying pan. Heat well, season with salt and pepper. Serve garnished with fried egg. Offer Worcestershire sauce or tomato catsup.

HASH *Hachis*

This dish is made of leftovers, and you may use either boiled or roast meat for it.

Brown a large, diced onion in a pan with butter, add

flour, and dilute with stock or soup until the gravy is thick. Add chopped, pickled cucumbers, sugar, salt, paprika and a little wine or brandy, and coloring until it attains an even brown color. Add the finely ground meat and allow to boil up. Pour the hash onto a round dish and garnish with browned potatoes, placed round it in a circle.

When serving, add one fried egg per person.

PARSLEY HEARTS
Stegte Hjerter

2 hearts
Butter
Parsley

Cut the hearts lengthwise and remove the large sinews and veins, drain off the blood. Stuff the hearts with a mixture made of ¼ cup butter and one bunch of parsley, taken from the coarsest stalks. Sew the hearts together. Brown some butter in a pan, and sear the hearts in it. Add a pinch of salt and enough water to cover half of the hearts. Allow to simmer over low heat for 3 hours, turning them at the halfway point. Take up just before serving and remove the thread. Cut into slices (not too thin).

Thicken the gravy with flour stirred in cream. For extra flavor, which gives a delightful taste, add currant juice. Brown a tablespoon of sugar on a pan, until it becomes caramel, add a tablespoon butter and mix well. Shake in tiny, boiled, peeled potatoes. Serve with the hearts in the gravy.

FORCEMEAT (STUFFING)
Fars

Danish housewives can stretch the budget and still be praised for their culinary skill by using "Kødfars"– forcemeat. If the butcher does not have it, it can be made by following the recipe for Danish Meat Balls.

CABBAGE BALLS
Kaaldolmer

12 cabbage leaves (large sized)
Forcemeat
Butter
Flour
Coloring

Put the cabbage leaves in boiling water and let boil up. Remove from the water and drain off. Put a spoonful of good forcemeat in each cabbage leaf (see next page), then roll the leaves round the meat and tie tightly.

Brown, in a pot with plenty of butter, each cabbage ball all over and add a little salt water. Keep over very low heat for about 30 minutes, and test with a knitting needle to see if the meat is well done and the cabbage tender.

Thicken the gravy with a paste made of flour and

water, and, if desired, add a little meat stock. Add a few drops of coloring to the gravy to make it an even brown color. Serve the cabbage balls in a deep dish with the gravy poured over.

DANISH MEAT BALLS
Frikadeller

½ lb. veal	Pepper to taste
½ lb. pork	1 grated onion
2 cups milk	2 tablespoons
1 egg	flour or 1 cup
Salt to taste	breadcrumbs

Put veal and pork together through a grinder 4 or 5 times. Add flour or breadcrumbs, milk, egg, onion, salt and pepper. Mix thoroughly. Drop on frying pan from a large tablespoon and fry over low heat.
Serve with browned butter, potatoes and stewed cabbage.

STUFFED WHITE CABBAGE
Fyldt Hvidkaal

1 large head of cabbage
Salt to taste
Forcemeat

Take a firm head of cabbage, and remove the outer leaves. Cut a "lid" from the stalk end, and hollow out the head until there is a shell left about the thickness of four or five leaves. Now fill with the same meat mixture as that used for the meat balls (above). As the meat will expand while cooking it is necessary to make provision for this when filling the cabbage.
Now put the cabbage lid on again and tie the head

together with a cotton thread. Put it into a pot with plenty of boiling, slightly salted water, and simmer for about 3½ hours.

Remove the thread and the lid and place the head on to a heated dish, open side down.

Serve with melted butter, or a sauce made of butter, flour and water which the cabbage was cooked in.

CAULIFLOWER MUSHROOM *Blomkaals Paddehat*

Clean a whole and large cauliflower and remove the leaves. Put it in boiling water, add salt and cook for five minutes. A layer of forcemeat, making a circle, is put on a piece of white cloth, sprinkled with flour. Place the cauliflower over this with the top downwards and gather the cloth together, making sure that the meat completely covers the cauliflower. Tie the cloth round the cauliflower and meat, put it back in boiling water and allow to simmer for another 20 minutes until the cauliflower is tender. The best way of testing it is with a knitting needle.

Before serving, take off the cloth carefully. Put the cauliflower à la mushroom on a hot dish, with the top upwards, of course. If desired, garnish the "mushroom" at the last minute with tiny pieces of hard-boiled egg yolk—to make it look like the "spots" on a mushroom.

Tomato sauce or melted butter may be served with it.

OPEN SANDWICHES
Smørrebrød

There is no doubt that Denmark's open sandwiches *(smørrebrød)* are the most famous feature of the Danish kitchen. Strangely enough they are not found elsewhere, even in neighbouring countries. Danish sandwiches have hundreds of variations and new ones are constantly being composed. From the simple, "flat", four sandwiches that office workers take with them to work and eat at their desks accompanied by a bottle of milk, they range to the gloriously colored "high" compositions, so generous that three are enough for a meal, eaten at restaurants. With the latter, piled high with good things, we drink Danish beer, which is exported to nearly every country in the world. With *smørrebrød* too we drink Danish *snaps*, a clear, innocent-looking fluid to be treated with respect. Though few really enjoy the taste, it has the power to make you feel happier, to loosen your tongue, to banish your inhibitions and to make social occasions an unqualified success.

Recipes for some typical Danish sandwiches follow. In Denmark we usually make them with dark rye bread. The bread should be made with the whole grain and should be as firm as possible, so that the slices can be quite thin. Also white bread can be used, but it should be with a heavy texture and it may be toasted. Fish is usually the starter and from there one goes to the meat and salad. Almost inevitably Danes wind up the *smørrebrød* meal with a piece of buttered white bread on which a good cheese has been placed.

FINE PICKLED HERRINGS *Fine marinerede Sild*

Clean, skin and bone six large salt herrings and soak them overnight in milk. Make a dressing of ¼ cup tarragon vinegar and ¼ cup ordinary vinegar sweetened with ½ cup sugar. Add 1 chopped onion, 1 chopped cooked carrot, two chopped pickled gherkins and 1 cup tomato ketchup and season with 10 whole cloves and 10 whole peppercorns. Let the dressing stand overnight.

Rinse the herrings, cut in slices and let them stand in the dressing 24 hours before serving.

Drain the herring pieces well before putting them on buttered bread, otherwise it might become soggy. Decorate with some of the onion from the dressing.

EGGS AND HERRINGS *Æg og Sild*

Spread slices of hard boiled egg on buttered bread and place one or more boned herrings lengthwise on the egg – or use Danish caviar as on photo by p. 49.

CHOPPED EGG AND HERRING *Hakket Æg og Sild*

Skin and bone two smoked herrings carefully. Boil two eggs until hard and put in a glass or large cup together with the herrings.

Run a sharp knife quickly from side to side until the ingredients are finely chopped and thoroughly mixed. Press the mixture on to buttered bread and top with cress. Makes 4 sandwiches.

SMOKED HERRINGS AND EGG YOLKS
Røget Sild med Æggeblomme

Butter the bread and top with long, cleaned fillets of smoked herrings.

Make a cavity in the center of the fillets with your fingers, circle it with a ring of raw onion, and put a raw egg yolk in it. Pile raw onions or chopped radishes at both ends of the yolk.

SHRIMP SANDWICH *Rejemad*

The small Danish shrimps are extremely popular delicacies and most Danish housewives are virtual masters at peeling them, but it is slow work for the beginner. At restaurants shrimps are always served peeled unless the customer specifically asks for unpeeled ones.

Put eventually a fresh leaf of lettuce on the buttered bread and top abundantly with cold boiled shrimps. (See illustration on opposite page).

Opposite: Open Sandwiches.
Eggs and Danish caviar, page 48,
H. C. Andersen Sandwich, page 55,
Shrimp Sandwich, page 49,
Blue Cheese and Egg yolk, page 56.
Sandwiches is also made with cold roastbeef, preferably with Tartar sauce.

SMOKED SALMON AND SCRAMBLED EGG
Røget Laks og Røræg

Put a piece of fresh smoked salmon on buttered bread, and on top of that, diagonally across the bread, a strip of cold scrambled egg. Decorate with finely chopped green dill.

LOBSTER SALAD *Hummersalat*

Mix small pieces of cold but freshly cooked lobster and asparagus in mayonnaise seasoned with tarragon vinegar. Put a lettuce leaf on each piece of buttered bread and spread with the mixture. Garnish with an extra piece of lobster and one or two asparagus tips. Serve immediately.

SMOKED EEL AND SCRAMBLED EGG
Røget Aal og Røræg

Cut smoked eel in 2-inch pieces. Remove skin and back bone. Put enough pieces of eel on a piece of buttered bread to cover it completely. Top with slices of cold scrambled egg and sprinkle with chives.

FRIED ROE *Ristet Torskerogn*

Put boiled cod roe under pressure until cold and cut in ½ inch slices with a sharp knife. Fry the slices in plenty of butter, place on buttered bread with a lemon slice on top. Cut the lemon slice half way and twist so it will stand upright.

FRIED FISH FILLETS *Stegt Fiskefilet*

As the fried fish fillet (of plaice or sole) should be served warm, do not place it on the bread as this would melt the butter.
Serve buttered bread on a separate plate. Serve with Tartar sauce.

HERRING SALAD
Sildesalat

Cooked meat	Salted and smoked or pickled herring
Cold potatoes	Sour mustard
Red beets	Flour
1 sliced onion	Butter

Place the meat, potatoes, red beets, onion, and well soaked herring on a chopping board together with the mustard and dice until the whole thing has become a mushy mass. If it is too dry and won't stick together add a little vinegar from the red beets, and flavor with sugar.
This procedure makes the "fine herring salad" usually made by the Danish housewife for everyday use. But you can make the salad coarse too by cutting (instead of dicing) the different ingredients in a long narrow strips and blending them with a thick sauce, made of 2 tablespoons butter and 4 cups flour cooked together and diluted with water or stock. Flavor the sauce with vinegar from the red beets, sugar and mustard to taste, and, if necessary, add a few drops of coloring until you get a beautiful red shade.

Spread the bread with the herring salad and decorate with slices of hard boiled egg, if you don't prefer topping it with a fried egg.

ITALIAN SALAD *Italiensk Salat*

Mix together cooked diced carrots, finely cut asparagus, small peas and mayonnaise. If home-made mayonnaise is used, add a few drops of tarragon vinegar just before stirring in the vegetables.

Press a lettuce leaf as tightly as possible on buttered bread and put a thick layer of Italian salad on top; decorate with tomato slices and cress.

TOMATO AND EGG *Tomat og Æg*

On one half of a piece of buttered bread place slices of hard boiled egg. On the other half arrange slices of tomato.

Garnish with cress.

TOMATO WITH RAW ONION *Tomat med raa Løg*

Top the buttered bread with several slices of tomato and put a pile of finely chopped, raw onions in the center.

ROAST BEEF AND FRIED EGG *Bøf med Spejlæg*

Place tender slices of cold roast beef on buttered bread. Fry onions in deep fat until brown and crisp and spread a layer of these on each slice of beef.

Top with fried eggs and serve before the egg cools. (Danish fried eggs are never turned).

RAW BEEF AND EGG *Tartar med Æg*

Scrape a piece of raw beef, preferably very fresh, off the sinews with a sharp knife and put a ½ inch layer on a piece of buttered bread.

Make a hollow in the center of the meat, circle it with a ring of raw onion, and place a raw egg yolk in the center. Put small piles of raw, chopped onions, shredded horseradish, capers, and pickles at each end.

HAM AND SCRAMBLED OR FRIED EGG
Skinke med Røræg eller Spejlæg

Butter the bread and spread it with a piece of lean boiled ham. Top it either with a strip of scrambled egg, sprinkled with finely cut chives, or with a freshly fried, warm egg.

HAM, PIGEON BREAST AND MUSHROOMS
Skinke med Duebryst

Butter a piece of dark rye bread and top with a good sized slice of ham. Add ½ or whole pigeon's breast cut nicely off the breastbone, and top the whole thing with stewed mushrooms and a thin slice of home-made liver paste.

LIVER PASTE I *Leverpostej I*

Put 1 lb. liver through the grinder together with 2 onions. Put 1 lb. fat pork twice through the grinder. Mix fat and liver with 1 tablespoon salt and 1 tablespoon pepper. Put in a fireproof dish and bake in a slow oven for 1 hour. The paste must not become too dark on top.

Put thick layers of cold paste on buttered bread. In winter the Danes put some rolls of fried bacon and a few stewed mushrooms on top or a slice of pickled red beet, and in summer a small dish of fresh cucumber salad is served so that you can put some of this on top yourself. Don't do it until the last minute, however, or both cucumber and liverpaste may become soggy.

LIVER PASTE II *Leverpostej II*

Put 2 lb. pig's liver twice through the grinder. Then put 1 lb. fat pork twice through the grinder together with an onion but do not mix the liver with the pork. Mix ¼ cup butter, ¼ cup flour and 2 cups of milk in a pot and let simmer. Add the ground pork and stir until the pork fat has melted. Take the pot off, add the liver and two whole eggs, 1 tablespoon salt and 1 teaspoon pepper.

Put in a fireproof dish, place this in water, and bake in a slow oven for 1½ hours.

COLD ROAST PORK *Flæskesteg*

Spread thin slices of roast pork on buttered bread and decorate with crisp pieces of rind, slices of jellied consommé (like consommé but with enough gelatine added to make it hold shape) cucumber salad (see page 28) or slices of pickled gherkin and red beets or red cabbage.

BOILED BREAST OF BEEF *Kogt Oksebryst*

Spread the bread with butter and put on slices of boiled breast of beef. Decorate with a small pile of chopped pickles at one end and a pile of shredded horseradish at the other. For a center decoration use a slice of tomato, cut halfway through and twisted so it will stand upright.

SMOKED SALAMI AND BOILED POTATO
Spegepølse med kogte Kartofler

Put slices of salami on bread spread with either butter or spiced pork fat.
Arrange a row of slices of cold boiled potato along the center of the salami, and on top of them run a strip of finely cut, fresh chives.

THE HANS ANDERSEN SANDWICH
H. C. Andersen Sandwich

Butter a piece of either dark or light rye bread and put two rows of crisp bacon on top. Place ½ slice liver paste across one of the rows and tomato slices across the other. In winter the latter may be substituted by tomato purée. Top the tomato slices with scraped horseradish and a strip of jellied consommé (see Cold Roast Pork). (See ill. by p. 49).

"THE VETERINARIANS'S MIDNIGHT SNACK"
Dyrlægens Natmad

Spread spiced lard on a piece of dark ryebread, and put slices of liver paste on top. Pieces of jellied consommé are placed over this, and on top pieces of slightly salted boiled veal. Decorate with cress.

BLUE CHEESE AND EGG YOLK
Roquefort Ost med Æggeblomme

Butter a piece of white bread and put a slice of Danish blue cheese on top. Place a raw egg yolk in a tomato ring in the center.

When eating the sandwich, break the yolk and spread it across the cheese.

Thin slices of radish may be used to decorate this and other kinds of cheese sandwiches. (See illustration opposite page 49).

DESSERTS
Desserter

There is an old Danish saying that a man who likes sweets will make a good husband. If that is true, then Danish husbands generally must be something quite out of the ordinary, they love sweets and their wives never tire of finding something new to satisfy their sweet tooth.

VEILED COUNTRY LASS
Bondepige med Slør

4 cups grated rye bread
2 tablespoons sugar
1 teaspoon butter
Whipped cream
Applesauce
Jam or jelly

Mix the black bread, sugar, and butter in a frying pan, and fry over low heat until the bread is crisp. Take off and let the mixture cool.

Just before serving spread a layer of the mixture on a flat dish, cover with a layer of applesauce (see page 63), then spread another layer of the bread mixture, cover with another layer of applesauce, and finally the rest of the bread. Cover the top with a thick layer of whipped cream. If desired a layer of jam or jelly may be substituted for one layer of applesauce.

Opposite: Fruit Jelly with cream, see page 61, and Cones with whipped cream, page 58

CARAMEL DESSERT
Karamelrand

12 eggs, separated
3 cups sugar
4 cups boiling cream
$\frac{1}{2}$ teaspoon vanilla
Whipped cream
1 glass brandy
1$\frac{1}{4}$ cups water

First prepare a ring mold in the following manner: Melt 2$\frac{1}{2}$ cups sugar in a pan until golden brown. Pour a little of this caramel into the mold, and turn until it is lined with caramel. Mix the rest of caramel with the water and boil until caramel is dissolved.
Now beat the egg yolks and $\frac{1}{2}$ cup sugar. Gradually add the boiling cream and vanilla, stirring constantly. Stir until mixture has cooled off, then add the egg whites, beaten stiff. Now pour this mixture into the mold, which is prepared for it, and let simmer on a grill, about $\frac{1}{2}$ hour, until firm. Take off. Turn on to a platter. Mix the whipped cream and the brandy with sauce before serving.

CONES WITH WHIPPED CREAM
Kræmmerhuse med Flødeskum

1 cup flour
$^3/_5$ cup sugar
2$\frac{2}{3}$ cup butter
8 egg whites
Whipped cream
Jelly

Melt butter and stir in sugar and flour. Allow mixture to cool and fold in stiffy beaten egg whites. Drop from a teaspoon on to a hot, well greased cookie sheet with plenty of space between each mound. With the spoon spread each mound into a flat oblong cake. Bake quickly in a hot oven. While still hot and soft remove cakes from sheet and make into cones. These will keep for a long time in a metal cake box. Serve filled with whipped cream topped with jelly. These cones are usually served as a dessert or with Danish "afternoon coffee". (See ill. by p. 57).

LEMON DELIGHT
"Kan ikke lade være"

10 eggs
1 1/4 cups sugar
3 lemons
4 tablespoons plain gelatine or 15 leaves of gelatine
1/2 cup boiling water

Mix the egg yolks well with sugar. Dissolve gelatine in boiling water and add lemon juice and grated rind. Add to egg yolk and sugar mixture. Add the stiffly beaten egg whites and beat the mixture until it begins to set. Pour into a bowl which has been dipped in water and leave until set. This dessert is better if prepared a day before it is to be served. Serve covered with whipped cream.

POOR KNIGHTS
Arme Riddere

2 or 3 slices of white bread per person
Milk
Sugar
Cinnamon
2 eggs
Breadcrumbs

Dip the slices of bread in milk; springle with sugar and cinnamon. Turn them in the beaten egg and dip in the crumbs. Fry the slices in plenty of butter until golden brown. Serve spread with jam or jelly.

PANCAKES
Pandekager

3¾ cups flour
½ cup beer
2 cups milk

4 eggs, separated
Dash of salt
Dash of sugar
½ tablespoon butter

Mix flour and egg yolks. Add beer and milk, (the batter should be thin). Beat until smooth. Add sugar and salt. Fold in stiffly beaten egg whites.

Pour a little of the batter on to a well greased frying pan and tilt so that batter quickly covers bottom of pan evenly.

Cook until golden brown on one side, then turn and cook on other side. (Toss like flapjack or use turner or spatula). Serve steaming hot with sugar or strawberry jam. Alternatively these pancakes are especially good wrapped around a lump of ice cream.

DANISH DOUGHNUTS
Æbleskiver

2 cups flour
½ teaspoon salt
2 cups buttermilk
1 teaspoon baking powder
2 eggs, separated
1 teaspoon sugar

Danish doughnuts are baked on top of the stove in a special pan with a hole for each doughnut.

Mix flour, salt and sugar. Beat together buttermilk and egg yolks, and add the flour mixture. Add baking powder and fold in stiffly beaten egg whites .Heat the pan and put melted butter in each hole. Pour batter into holes but do not quite fill them. Place over low heat and turn quickly when half done. Serve very hot with jelly or applesauce (see page 63).

RICE FRITTERS
Klatkage af Risengrød

Cold boiled rice
2 eggs
Raisins

Grated lemon rind
Chopped almonds
2 tablespoons flour
Butter

Mix the ingredients – the rice, eggs, raisins, grated lemon rind, chopped almonds and flour. Drop by spoonful onto a hot buttered frying pan; fry on both sides. Sprinkle with sugar and serve with jam.

FRUIT JELLY WITH CREAM
Rødgrød med Fløde

$1\frac{2}{3}$ lbs. red currants
$1\frac{2}{3}$ lbs. raspberries
8 cups water
$\frac{1}{2}$ cup potato flour (or corn-flour)
Vanilla
Cut almonds

The foreigner who visits Denmark remembers this dessert mainly because its Danish name is almost impossible for him to pronounce. His Danish friends are always greatly amused by his effort to say it right. It is a popular dish on a hot summer day.

Wash the currants and raspberries, add water and boil. When all the juice has boiled out, remove the berries, force through a fine sieve or a cloth, and put the juice back into the pot. Sweeten to taste, and thicken with the potato flour or corn-flour, using $\frac{1}{4}$ cup to every 4 cups of juice. If potato flour is used, be sure to have juice boiling hot when it is added, and to take the juice off the stove while adding the flour. If potato flour boils, the jelly will be "long" – a sure sign of a bad cook in Denmark!

Add the vanilla. While still hot pour into a glass bowl. When it begins to stiffen decorate the surface with a pattern of blanched almonds. Serve with sugar and cream. (See illustration opposite page 57).

RHUBARB DESSERT
Rabarbergrød

2½ lbs. rhubarb
³/₅ cup sugar
1 teaspoon vanilla extract
¼ cup potato flour
　(or corn-flour)

It is best to make this rhubarb dessert early in the season when the stalks are young and tender—then it is not necessary to strain them. Cut the rhubarb into half-inch pieces and put into a pot with just enough water to cover. Add sugar and simmer until the stalks are mushy. Add vanilla and if necessary a little more sugar to taste and thicken with ¼ cup potato flour per quart. (Be sure to have juice boiling hot, but do not cook, when adding potato flour). Then sprinkle with a little sugar and serve with cream.

STRAWBERRIES AND CREAM
Jordbær med Fløde

Strawberries
Sugar
Cream

In Denmark we eat our strawberries in deep dishes (like soup plates), we sprinkle the whole berries with sugar and pour cream over them. Whether or not you find this strange depends on your nationality – it always amazes both the French and the Swiss.

DANISH APPLESAUCE
Æblegrød

3 lbs. apples
½ cup water
Sugar to taste

Applesauce is another typical Danish summer dessert. Peel and quarter the apples, and carefully remove cores. Add the water, and cook over very low heat until the apples are soft. Now mash them a little, and sweeten to taste. Pour into a glass bowl. Serve with cream and sugar.

APPLE CAKE
Æblekage

2 lbs. cooking apples
1 cup melted butter
Sugar
Dried breadcrumbs
Jelly
Whipped cream
Vanilla

Peel, core and quarter apples. Simmer, covered, in a little water until soft. Force through a sieve and sweeten to taste. Add vanilla.

Butter a fireproof dish, put layers of breadcrumbs and layers of applesauce in the dish alternately, letting the bottom and the top layers be of breadcrumbs.Pour the melted butter down through the applecake, and bake for 30 minutes in a hot oven. Turn onto a plate and decorate with jelly and whipped cream.

Additional whipped cream may be served in a separate dish. Serve the cake either hot or cold. (See illustration opposite page 64).

CAKES AND PASTRIES
Kager

Danish cakes and cookies are so rich and artistic that they deserve the place of honor they receive on the coffee table and, together with the many other kinds of sweets for dessert, they are often to be found in the dining room.

CREAM TARTS	2 cups flour	*Cream filling:*
Linser	$1^1/_8$ cup butter	1 cup milk
	3 tablespoons caster sugar	1 tablespoon sugar
		$^1/_8$ cup potato flour
	2 egg yolks	2 eggs
		Vanilla

Sift and mix flour and sugar, combine with the cold butter and egg yolks. Knead the dough lightly and let it rise in a cool place for about 20 minutes. Meanwhile make the filling. Mix eggs, flour and sugar. Boil the milk for a few minutes, add vanilla and beat in egg mixture. Bring to the boil again beating constantly. Take off and pour into a bowl. Stir occasionally to prevent the forming of skin. Roll the dough into a thin sheet and line the cups of

Cakes and Danish pastry, among these:
Cream Tarts, see page 64,
Jewish cakes, page 66,
Almond Rings, page 67,
Danish pastry, page 68,
Apple Cake, page 63

a muffin tin with it. Put a tablespoon of the cooled filling in each cup. Cover with a lid of the dough and firmly press the edge. Bake 15-20 minutes in a hot oven. (See illustration opposite page 64).

VANILLA RINGS
Vaniljekranse

3¾ cup flour
1¼ cup sugar
1¾ cup butter
1 egg
4 oz. scalded, minced almonds
Vanilla

Work all the ingredients together and let the dough stand for 20 minutes. Then put it into a pastry bag or tube and press out into a long thin roll. Cut the roll in small pieces and form into small rings on a well-greased tin. Bake until light brown.

BROWN COOKIES
Brunekager

1 cup almonds
Orange peel or lemon peel
1 teaspoon cinnamon
½ teaspoon ground ginger
½ teaspoon ground cloves

2 cups dark syrup
1 cup brown sugar
½ cup butter

1 tablespoon baking powder
6 cups flour
Almonds for decoration

Mix syrup, sugar and butter and bring to the boil. Take off and add baking powder, flour, chopped almonds, orange peel, cinnamon, ginger and cloves. Blend well with a spoon until smooth. Let the dough stand for 1-3 days, then knead thoroughly on the baking board – use flour if it sticks. Roll out very thin, cut into round cakes with a wineglass and place on buttered cookie sheet. Brush with egg white and decorate with half an almond. Bake in a moderate oven until brown and crisp.

JEWISH CAKES
Jødekager

2½ cups flour
1 cup butter
¾ cup sugar
1 egg
1 teaspoon salt of hartshorn

Mix well flour, butter, sugar, salt of hartshorn and egg. Chill. Roll the dough out very thin and cut with wineglass into round cakes.

Place the cakes close together on a buttered baking sheet. Brush with beaten egg white and sprinkle with mixed cinnamon and sugar and cut almonds. Bake in a moderate oven until light brown. (See ill. by page 64).

CHRISTMAS CRULLERS
Klejner

3 eggs
¾ cup sugar
3¾ cups flour
3 tablespoons cream
⅔ cup butter
Grated rind of 1 lemon
Deep fat

Mix eggs, sugar, rind and melted butter and add 3 tablespoons of cream and 1 lb flour. Knead into a smooth dough. Roll it out very thin and cut into long, narrow strips with slanting ends. Make a slit in the center of each strip, put one of the ends through the slit, making a knot in the center. Fry in hot deep fat until light brown and drain on brown paper. Do not allow crullers to touch each other while frying.

LOVE RINGS
Kærlighedskranse

4 egg yolks (hard boiled)
3 cups flour
½ lb. butter
¼ lb. sugar
Vanilla

Blend the yolks and the sugar, cream in the butter, add the flour and vanilla. Mix the whole thing well and let the dough stand in a cool place for about one hour. Then roll it into thin strips, cut into pieces of equal size and make them into small doughnut shaped rings. Do not put them too close to each other on the pan as they swell while baking. Bake until golden brown.

ALMOND RINGS
Kransekage

1 lb. almonds
1 oz. bitter almonds
3 cups sugar
4 egg whites

Put the blanched almonds through grinder twice. Add sugar and egg whites and mix well. When smooth place in a pot over slow heat until warm. Shape dough into 1–inch diameter rolls, press gently with fingers to give form of a roof. Form into rings and place on well buttered and floured baking sheet. Bake in a slow oven until light brown. When cooled

decorate with frosting made of 1 egg white, ¾ cup
icing sugar, ½ tablespoon vinegar or lemon juice.
Mix well for 10—15 min. until smooth and force
through fine paper tube to make zig-zag lines, both
on inside and outside of the rings. (See ill. by p. 64).

SANDCAKE
Sandkage

1¼ cup butter
1¼ cup sugar
3 eggs
1 cup flour
1 cup potato flour
⅙ cup rice flour
1 teaspoon vanilla extract

Mix the butter and sugar, add the eggs one at a time,
and finally the sifted flour and vanilla extract. Bake
in a moderate oven about 1 hour, or until golden
brown. If baked only 45 min. the cake will be under-
done but tastier.

DANISH PASTRY
Dansk Wienerbrød

4 cups flour
1 teaspoon salt
¼ cup sugar
2 yeast cakes (2¼ oz.)
1 cup milk
1 egg
1½ cup butter

Sift flour and mix with sugar and salt. Mix yeast
with a little cold milk. Add this, the rest of the milk
and the beaten egg to flour and sugar. Beat well until
smooth with a wooden spoon.
Roll out the dough on baking board to 1 finger
thickness. Spread small pieces of butter on ⅔ of the

dough. The butter must have same consistency as the dough; if it is too soft it melts into the dough.

Fold together into three layers like folding a napkin, first the part without butter. Roll out and fold again. Repeat three or four times.

Leave in cold place ½ hour. This is the dough with which many different kinds of Danish pastry is made. When pastry is shaped, place on baking sheet and leave in cold place to rise for 15–20 min., then brush with egg white and bake in a fast oven until golden brown. (See illustration opposite page 64).

Cocks' Combs (Hanekamme). Roll out dough to ½ finger thickness and spread with a paste made of equal parts of butter and sugar, then cut into square pieces 4" × 4". Place filling across middle and fold over. Press the edges firmly together and make 4–5 deep slashes in this side. Let rise, brush with egg white and spread with chopped almonds and sugar.

Spandauers. Roll our dough, spread with paste and cut as above. Place filling in middle. Fold corners to the center and press down. After baking drop 1 teaspoon of jelly in the center and spread with frosting of icing sugar and water.

Chocolate Buns (Crèmeboller). Roll out dough, spread with paste and cut as above. Place filling of vanilla crème in middle, fold corners to the center, forming dough as a ball and place upside down on baking sheet. After baking spread with frosting of icing sugar, cocoa and water.

As filling may be used apple sauce, jelly, prunes, vanilla creme or almond paste:

Vanilla Creme. Mix 1 egg yolk, 1 tablespoon sugar, 1 tablespoon flour and ¾ cup milk and cook until thick. Take off, add ½ teaspoon vanilla extract and cool stirring occasionally.

Almond Paste. Cream ½ cup butter, add ¼ lb. ground, blanched almonds and ½ cup sugar and mix well until smooth. Another kind of almond paste without butter is made of: ¼ lb. almonds, ½ cup sugar and 3 egg whites. Work well together until smooth.

———————

WEIGHTS AND MEASURES

1 cup liquid: 2¼ decilitres
1 cup butter: ½ lb. or 225 grams
1 cup flour: 4½ oz. or 125 grams
1 cup sugar: 7   oz. or 200 grams

INDEX
English

★ *Open Sandwiches.*

Danish

The photographs in this book are by Heini Egli (opposite page 16 and 32), Niels Elswing (opposite page 49 and 57). The photograph on the frontispiece and opposite page 64 are by Vagn Guldbrandsen by kind permission of the Danish Agriculture Marketing Board.